Table of Contents

INTRODUCTION

Nowadays, we feel like time is running through our hands like water, and we simply don't have time to do things we would have leisurely enjoyed doing a decade ago. We simply don't have the time to cook healthy and tasty meals for ourselves and our families, and because of this, we end up relying on prepacked meals. Pre-packaged meals are filled with sodium, processed carbohydrates, sugars, saturated fats, and a lot of preservatives, and none of these things are good for your body. Eating processed foods frequently can cause severe damage to your body and is the leading cause of many diseases, such as liver failure and type 2 diabetes.

When people realize that processed foods are unhealthy, they do tend to find healthier alternatives like meal kits. However, meal kits also pose a huge problem since they aren't very budget and environment-friendly. The meal kits also take a significant amount of time to put together, and even though there are proportioned ingredients, you still have to cut the vegetables and meat and assemble the recipe while reading the instructions. In addition to all of this, we are also experiencing an economic crisis, and the cost of food is through the roof simply because the production cannot keep up with the demand. A few months ago, the grocery bill would probably be 100 dollars or so, but now, it will cost you at least a couple of hundred to just get basic food items. With the cost of food rising, meal kits will probably get even more expensive and unreachable, and this is exactly why people need a better alternative to cooking. This is where the Ninja Foodi SmartLid 11-in-1 comes in! It is a crockpot, but instead of a typical crockpot lid, it is equipped with an air frying lid, fundamentally changing your cooking game. You no longer have to worry about putting tasty food on the table because this 11-in-1 contraption helps you cook a wide variety of meals in a very limited time.

The Ninja Foodie Multicooker 11-in-1 takes versatility to the next level and allows you to swap all your kitchen appliances for just one, saving you time, energy, and lots of counter space. So, if you want to learn how to use your Ninja Multicooker properly, keep reading!

Chapter 1: NINJA Foodi 11-in-1 SmartLid Multi-Cooker 6L [OL550UK]

Benefits Of The Ninja Foodi OL550UK

The Ninja Foodie 11-in-1 SmartLid cooker is a multicooker that allows you to air fry, steam, pressure cook, and much more. It comes equipped with an innovative combination steam function and is perfect for people who want to take their cooking to the next level without investing huge amounts of money in different appliances. However, this might not be enough to convince you to buy one, so here are some reasons you should consider choosing this Multicooker.

Easy To Clean

This Multicooker includes a 6L cooking pot that has a ceramic coating. All parts of the Ninja Foodi are dishwasher safe, so they are super easy to clean.

Large Capacity

This cooker has a capacity of 6L and 3.7 Cook and Crisp Basket, which is perfect for a family of four. You can easily make a 2 kg roast inside this fryer, and the large capacity of this cooker is one of its best features.

Cooking Functions

This one pot has 11 different functions, so it not only saves you tons of counter space and money, but it is also easy and convenient to have all your appliances merge into one.

Energy Saving

An average oven typically sues around 2kW, and this Multicooker only uses 1.76kW. In addition to that, the oven has a much longer surface area; it takes much longer to heat up, and this unit is small, so it takes a lot less time to heat up. This difference in voltage and area doesn't seem like much, but it can save up almost 65 percent on your energy bill.

Smartlid Slider

Unlock 11 functions and 3 modes and easily switch between combi-steam modes, air frying, and pressure cooking with the SmartLid slider.

Steam And Crisp

Create perfectly cooked chicken that is crispy on the outside and juicy and tender on the inside.

Air Frying Mode

This mode helps you crisp up the foods with little to no oil. In fact, this Ninja Foodi Multi-cooker can help you reduce up to 75 percent of your oil consumption. In this mode, you can create anything from juicy chicken to golden chips and vegetables. In addition to all of that, you can also choose a range of other convections and hob-style functions. you can sauté ingredients, create delicious sauces and caramelized onions, sear steaks to perfection, dehydrate ingredients, and so much more! The limit is your imagination.

Pressure Cook Mode

The pressure cooking mode can help you cook almost 70 percent faster than traditional cooking methods. This mode uses super-heated steam technology to

cook delicate meals and tenderize large cuts of meat in a fraction of the time so you can still enjoy homecooked meals without having to put in tons of time and effort.

Benefits Of the Ninja Foodi Multi-Cooker 11-In-1

There are numerous benefits of investing in a multicooker; here are some of them:

- Multicookers come equipped with unique cooking technologies, which means that you can cook much faster as compared to conventional cooking methods. For example, cooking corned beef can take you 8 hours in a slow cooker, five in an oven, and only one hour in a multicooker.

- Multicookers save you a lot of money, not only because you get so many appliances in one but also because multicookers use a lot less electricity, and this can help you save almost 65 percent on your electricity bills.

- Minimizing how much stuff you have on the counter space is essential, especially for smaller homes, since cluttered spaces can make your apartment look even smaller. Investing in a multicooker means that you won't need any other appliance, so that will free up a lot of counter and cupboard space.

- These appliances are also pretty easy to clean since all the parts can go inside the dishwasher, so you won't have to do any washing by hand.

People consider detaching the parts and cleaning them very tedious, but once you figure out what goes where it will only take a couple of minutes to take apart and reassemble the appliance.

- The Ninja Foodi is the perfect Multicooker because it not only lets you steam, pressure cook, and dehydrate your food, among many other things, but it also comes equipped with an air fryer lid which helps you cut down on your fat and oil consumption.

Parts And Accessories

There are a lot of parts to this 11-in-1 Ninja crockpot. Here are some of them:

- Reversible rack
- Cook and crisp basket
- 6L removable crockpot
- Cooker lid
- Smart lid slider
- DE attachable diffuser
- Control panel
- Cooker base
- Lid handle
- Condensation collector
- Pressure release valve
- Vent and seal
- Air outlet vent
- Anti-clog cap

Control Panel

There are a lot of functions within this crockpot so let's discuss them and what you can achieve with them.

Cooking Functions

• Keep Warm

When you are using the slow cook, pressure cook, or steam cycle, the cooker will automatically settle at Keep Warm at the end of the cycle to keep your food fresh. You can press the Keep Warm button again at the end of the cycle to disable this automatic transition.

• Air Fry

Air frying can help you lower the amount of oil you are consuming and results in crispy and crunchy food that is even better in taste and texture than traditional deep frying.

Dehydrate

The dehydrating function can help you dehydrate meats, fruits, and vegetables and turn them into healthy snacks.

• Pressure Cooking

This function allows you to quickly cook food while maintaining tenderness.

• Steam Bake

Now you can easily bake fluffy and tasty cakes and other kinds of sweets in your crockpot.

• Steam Air Fry

Use the Ninja's sophisticated seam air frying technique to crisp up your meats and vegetables without having to use oil.

• Bake

This modern countertop appliance can be converted into an over, so you won't have to spend a lot of money buying other appliances since the Ninja crockpot can allow you to bake delicious and fluffy cakes easily.

• Grill

This crockpot allows you to easily eat grilled meat and caramelize and brown your food without having to use an outdoor grill and also without standing in the smoke and heat.

• Sear/Sauté

You can easily brown meats, sauté vegetables, make sauces, and so much more in this ninja 11-in-1 crockpot.

• Slow Cook

Cook your food for a longer period of time at a much lower temperature to achieve tasteful and rich soups, curries, and so much more.

• Yogurt

This Ninja appliance allows you can make your own yogurt at home by helping you pasteurize and ferment the milk.

• Steam

Gently cook delicate foods at higher temperatures without losing taste or texture.

Operating Buttons

• Smartlid Slider

As you move the slider, the available functions in each mode will be visible so you can easily choose your desired mode.

• Dial

Once you figure out which mode you want to use, utilize the dial to scroll through all the available functions until you reach your desired one.

• Left Arrow

Use this arrow to choose the cooking temperature. These buttons will also set the internal outcome when using the Manual or Preset buttons.

• Right Arrow

Press the right arrow to choose the appropriate cooking time.

• Start/Stop

Press this option to start the cooking, and if you want to stop any time during cooking, press the same button, and the cooking process will pause.

• Power

This button allows you to turn the appliance on and off.

Using The Ninja Foodi Smartlid Multi-Cooker 11-In-1

Setting Up the Air Fryer

- Remove the product from its packaging and remove all the stickers and tape.
- Read the warnings, instructions, and important safeguards to avoid any personal injury or property damage.
- Wash the silicone ring, cook and crisp basket, removable cooking pot, condensation collector, and reversible rack

in warm, soapy water, then rinse and dry thoroughly. Do not clean the appliance itself in the dishwasher since it isn't waterproof and will short-circuit.

- The silicone ring is reversible and can be put in any direction. Insert the silicone ring on the underside of the lid and fix it on the outer edges of the ring rack. Make sure the ring is flat and fully in place before using the lid.

- Install the condensation collector into its slot at the base of the cooker. Remember to empty the water collected inside after each use.

- The anti-clog cap protects the inner part of the pressure lid from clogging and potential food splatter. It should be cleaned with a cleaning brush after every use.

- To remove the anti-clog cap, firmly hold it between your thumb and index finger and rotate your hand clockwise. To reinstall, position it back in place and press down. Always make sure that your anti-clogging cap is correctly installed before use.

Using The Pressure-Cooking Functions

- Before using the pressure-cooking function on actual food, it is recommended that first-time users use water to test and familiarize themselves with pressure cooking.

- Place the pot inside the base of the cooker and add almost 700ml of water, making sure that the water is at room temperature.

- Close the lid and mode the SmartLid slider, so it is in the pressure position.

- Make sure that the pressure release valve is sealed. The valve is loose when it is fully installed.

- This Multicooker will default to high pressure when it starts, so use the right arrow to adjust the time and press start to begin.

- The display will show "PrE' to indicate that the pressure is building inside the unit, and when the cooker is fully pressurized, the counter will start counting down.

- When the cooking time is completed, the timer will beep and then automatically start releasing the pressure. There will

be a warning chime before the pressure valve opens, and when it does, the steam will start escaping from the chamber. As soon as the display shows "open lid," move the slider to the right and unlock the lid.

- If you don't immediately open the lid, the machine will automatically switch on the keep warm mode.

Using the Combi-Steam Functions

Steam Air Fry

- In this setting, the position of the pressure release valve doesn't matter, and it could be in either position.

- Fit the Cook and Crisp Basket or the reversible rack inside the pot. Add your ingredients inside, and then add some water so there is enough liquid to create steam.

- Close the lid and move the slider to Combi-Steam Mode and use the dial to select the Steam Air Fry function.

- The machine will default to a preset time and temperature, so it utilizes the up and down arrows to get your desired settings.

- Once you are happy with the setting, press Start to begin the cooking process.

- The pressure will build inside the chamber, and once it is fully pressurized, the timer will start.

- When the cooking time is completed, the machine will beep.

- If you want to add additional time, then use the arrows to add more. And because the unit is already hot, the machine will skip the preheating and get right to cooking.

Steam Bake

- The Steam Bake function is very similar to the Steam Air Fry. The only difference is that you need to place the reversible rack inside the machine. Then, add tin foil at the bottom of the reversible rack and add water to create the steam.

- Move the slider to Combi-Steam and select the Steam function. Choose your settings and press start.

- Once it is done, the machine will stop and beep, indicating that the process is complete.

Using Air Fry and HOB Functions

Dehydrate

- Place the reversible rack inside in the lower position and place a layer of ingredients on the rack.
- Move the SmartLid slider to the Air Fry/HOB function and then choose Dehydrate. Adjust your temperature and time and start the process.

Sear/Sauté

- Add the food inside the pit and move the slide to the Air Fry/HOB and select the Seat/Sauté function.
- The default setting will display, so use the up and down arrow to select between LO 1, 2, 3, 4, and HI 5. Unfortunately, you can't adjust the time when using this particular function.
- The good thing about this set is that you can use it with the lid open and closed/
- Press Start/Stop to begin the cooking process.
- Only use utensils that are suitable for non-stick surfaces inside the cooking pot. Do not use metal since it will scratch the non-stick coating.

Slow Cook

- Add the food inside the pot and fill till the max line. Next, move the slider to the Air Fry/HOB function and choose slow cook.
- The machine will set to the default setting, so use the arrows to choose between HI, LO, and BUFFET."
- Use the up and down buttons to adjust the cooking time and press Start.
- Adjust the cooking time in 15-minute increments for up to 12 hours.
- When cooking is finished, the machine will automatically switch to "keep warm."

Cleaning and Maintenance

- The machine needs to be properly cleaned after each use.
- Unplug the machine from the socket and remove the cooker base and the rack inside the machine.
- Clean the cooker base and the control panel with a clean, damp cloth.
- The cooking pot, reversible silicone ring, rack, and Cook and Crisp Basket can be washed in the dishwasher.
- The pressure release valve and anti-clogging ap can be washed with mild dish soap and warm water.
- If food is stuck to the pots and racks, submerge them in warm soapy water. Do not use an abrasive pad. If scrubbing is required, use a nylon pad with mild liquid dish soap.
- To remove the silicone ring, gently pull it outwards, section by section, from the silicone ring rack.
- The ring can be installed on either side, so there is no right side. To reinstall, press the rig back into the silicone rack section by section.
- Wash the silicone ring with warm water or dishwater. It is pretty common

for the ring to absorb some smells from certain acidic foods. This is exactly why it is advised that you buy an alternative silicone ring, just in case.

- Never pull the silicone ring aggressively out of the ring rack since this can cause the ring to deform and affect the pressure sealing functions.

- If your silicone ring has cracks, cuts, or any other damage, you need to replace it immediately.

Frequently Asked Questions

Question: How do I put the seal back in place?

Answer: Putting the seal back in place is a bit of a learning curve, but generally, if the seal is freshly washed and warm, it is easier to wiggle it back into place.

Question: Is the inner pot stainless steel?

Answer: The inside of the pot has a ceramic coating, so it is stainless. As a result, the pot is incredibly versatile and easy to clean and use.

Question: Can you put foil inside the Ninja Foodie Multi-Cooker?

Answer: Yes, you can use foil inside the cooker without any problems. In fact, it might be a good idea to use foil since it absorbs a lot of heat and cooks the food even faster.

Question: Does the 11-in-1 Ninja Foodi come with a rice cooker function?

Answer: You can do almost anything with this Multicooker. Even though it doesn't specifically have a rice cooking function, and you might need to experiment with the setting depending on the amount of food you are cooking, you can easily figure out the perfect settings for cooking food.

Question: Could you fit a chicken inside the Ninja?

Answer: You can easily fit a 2kg chicken inside the Ninja Foodi 11-in-1, and by the end of the cooking process, you will have a crispy, juicy chicken.

Chapter 2: Breakfast

Air Fryer French Toast

Prep Time: 10 Minutes
Cook Time: 10 Minutes   Serves: 4

Ingredients:

- 4 slices medium thickness bread
- 2 eggs
- 80ml milk
- 40ml double cream (optinal)
- 1 tsp cinnamon
- 1 tsp vanilla extract
- Optional toppings (berries, icing sugar, maple syrup)

Directions:

1. Slice the bread into halves, quarters or lengthwise into soldiers and lay flat in a shallow dish (you may need to do this in batches).
2. Whisk the eggs with the milk, cream (if using), cinnamon and vanilla extract.
3. Pour the egg mixture over the bread and leave to soak for a few minutes, turning it over halfway.
4. While the bread is soaking, preheat the air fryer to 180°C.
5. Carefully transfer the soaked bread to the cook basket and air fry for 8 to 10 minutes, turning halfway.
6. If at the end of the air frying time the bread is not crisp enough, turn the temperature up to 200°C and air fry for a further 1 minute on each side.
7. Serve as it is or with some fresh berries, bananas, maple syrup or a sprinkling of icing sugar.

Nutritional Value (Amount per Serving):

Calories: 826; Fat: 45.76; Carb: 76.48; Protein: 29.08

Air Fryer Roast Potatoes

Prep Time: 5 Minutes
Cook Time: 30 Minutes   Serves: 3

Ingredients:

- 1/2 tbsp vegetable oil
- salt & pepper
- 600g potatoes

Directions:

1. Pre-heat the air fryer to 180°C.
2. Peel, wash and chop your potatoes.
3. Drizzle with the vegetable oil and salt and pepper.
4. Add to the cook basket.
5. Cook for 15 minutes at 180°C. Shake well.
6. If you're adding additional herbs, spices or seasonings now if the time to add these.
7. Cook for another 10 minutes at 180°C. Check. If required cook for a further 5 minutes.

Nutritional Value (Amount per Serving):

Calories: 180; Fat: 2.5; Carb: 36.43; Protein: 4.26

Air Fryer Mashed Potatoes

Prep Time: 5 Minutes
Cook Time: 25 Minutes   Serves: 3

Ingredients:

- 500 g baby potatoes first early works too
- 15 ml olive oil
- Salt and pepper
- 20 g butter
- 1 stalk chives

Directions:

1. Wash and dry your potatoes.

2.Place the potatoes on a piece of tin foil

3.Cover with 15ml of olive oil, sprinkle generously with salt and pepper. Wrap up the foil over the potatoes.

4.Air fryer at 200°C for 20 minutes.

5.Once the time is up ensure that the potatoes are fork tender. IF not then you'll want to cook for 3-5 minutes more.

6.Once your potatoes are cooked through remove and place in a bowl.

7.Add 20g of butter and mash until smooth.

8.Season with salt and pepper.

9.Chop a stalk of chives and scatter on the top.

10.If you're serving family style then smooth the top and dab 10g of butter on to give it a nice presentation.

Nutritional Value (Amount per Serving):

Calories: 427; Fat: 29.21; Carb: 37.18; Protein: 8.59

Air Fryer Cheese Biscuits

Prep Time: 4 Minutes
Cook Time: 10 Minutes   Serves: 6

Ingredients:

- 115 g self-raising flour
- 55 g butter or margarine
- Pinch of salt
- 35 g cheddar cheese grated
- 75 ml semi-skimmed milk

Directions:

1.Mix together the self-raising flour and butter.

2.Add a pinch of salt.

3.Add grated cheddar cheese.

4.Combine well.

5.Add the semi-skimmed milk and mix.

6.Divide the mixture into 6.

7.Line the cook basket with parchment paper.

8.Drop the mixture inside the cook basket.

9.Cook at 200°C for 8-10 minutes.

Nutritional Value (Amount per Serving):

Calories: 633; Fat: 36.13; Carb: 33.12; Protein: 43.12

Air Fryer Pizza

Prep Time: 5 Minutes
Cook Time: 10 Minutes   Serves: 1

Ingredients:

- 1 pizza base
- 1 serving of pizza sauce
- Toppings of your choice – We usually go for pepperoni or nduja sausage and mozzarella
- Dried herbs of your choice

Directions:

1. Spread your pizza sauce on your pizza base.
2. Add your toppings.
3. Sprinkle over some dried herbs (or fresh if you have them!). We freeze fresh herbs so we usually have some on hand, if not we use dried.
4. Lightly spray the cook basket to avoid sticking and then place the pizza inside.
5. Cook at 200°C for 8 minutes for a thin crust and 10 minutes for a deep pan/thick crust. Check the pizza 2-3 minutes before serving, as cooking times will vary based on the size of your air fryer, and the pizza itself of course!
6. If you fancy making mini pizzas I find that these just take 5-6 minutes, which is great if you're preparing an after school snack or just fancy something extra tasty with a glass of wine at the end of a long day!

Nutritional Value (Amount per Serving):

Calories: 1547; Fat: 52.24; Carb: 195.81; Protein: 73.6

Air Fryer Pizza Scrolls

Prep Time: 10 Minutes
Cook Time: 7 Minutes   Serves: 6

Ingredients:

- 1/2 portion of pizza dough see my recipe linked above
- 2 portions of roasted tomato pizza sauce see my recipe linked above
- 60 g grated mozzarella and cheddar mix
- Mixed Italian herbs basil and oregano

Directions:

1. Roll out the pizza dough as thin as possible.
2. Spread over the tomato pizza sauce.
3. Add the grated cheddar.
4. Sprinkle on 1/2 of your herbs.
5. Roll up as tightly as possible. I find that using baking paper or cling film works well here.
6. Slice into 2.5cm slices.
7. Pop into the cook basket.
8. Bake at 200°C for 6-7 minutes until golden brown.
9. Sprinkle over the remainder of the herbs when serving.

Nutritional Value (Amount per Serving):

Calories: 324; Fat: 11.27; Carb: 42.2; Protein: 9.79

Air Fryer Toast

Prep Time: 1 Minute
Cook Time: 4 Minutes   Serves: 4

Ingredients:

- Sliced bread of course! I normally use 4 slices of sourdough sliced white or brioche style bread for the tastiest results.
- That's it... Seriously. Surprising I know...! Probably my easiest ever of all

my air fryer recipes!

- Don't forget your favourite toast toppings too see above for some inspiration.

Directions:

1. Pre-heat the air fryer to 200°C for a couple of minutes.
2. Place the slices of bread into the cook basket. If you've got an air fryer oven with racks then use one of the lower racks to keep the bread away from the heating element.
3. The main aim is to ensure that you only have one layer of toast, to avoid blocking the air from flowing around the air fryer basket freely.
4. You don't need to use any olive oil, or spray oil, when making toast, like I might suggest with other air fryer recipes.
5. Cook for 3-4 minutes, turning once during the cooking time.
6. You may find that your air fryer distributes the air well enough not to really need to turn, but I like to ensure even cooking wherever I can! Especially as it just takes a few seconds with a pair of tongs.
7. Remove when golden brown. You can adjust the cooking time up or down based on your own preferred toasting. I like a medium – golden brown, which is what the cooking times in this recipe are based upon.

Nutritional Value (Amount per Serving):

Calories: 176; Fat: 7.43; Carb: 2.79; Protein: 24.28

Air Fryer Mashed Potato Balls

Prep Time: 5 Minutes
Cook Time: 15 Minutes   Serves: 2

Ingredients:

- 300 g of leftover mashed potato
- 1 egg
- 50 g of breadcrumbs homemade or packet are fine. If you want a different texture then consider some Panko breadcrumbs.
- Salt and pepper

Directions:

1. Take your leftover mashed potatoes.
2. Whisk one egg in a bowl. Season with salt and pepper.

3. Measure your breadcrumbs into a separate bowl.
4. Use a small ice cream scoop, or two tablespoons to roll your leftover mashed potato in small balls. The smaller the better to avoid them breaking up!
5. Once rolled dip the mashed potato balls into egg and then breadcrumbs.
6. Spray the cook basket with spray oil.
7. Add the mashed potato balls into the basket.
8. Cook at 200°C for 16 minutes. Check, and gently shake, at 5 minutes, then 10 minutes in, just to avoid the balls sticking to the bottom of the basket.
9. Serve with tomato ketchup and enjoy.

Nutritional Value (Amount per Serving):

Calories: 247; Fat: 5.46; Carb: 34.83; Protein: 9.17

Air Fryer Potato Wedges

Prep Time: 5 Minutes
Cook Time: 20 Minutes   Serves: 2

Ingredients:

- 400 g Potatoes
- Spray oil
- Optional dressings
- Garlic & parsley – mince together 2 garlic cloves 15g butter (melted) & 1 teaspoon chopped parsley
- Cajun seasoning I buy this from Tesco

Directions:

1. Preheat your air fryer to 160°C.   2. Wash potatoes, peel if desired.
3. Cut potatoes in half.   4. Then cut in to quarters.
5. Slice diagonally to make 3-4 wedges from each quarter.
6. Rinse in cold water.
7. Pat them dry on a clean towel or using kitchen towel.
8. Spray with oil and add your optional dressing, if required.
9. Alternatively you can use 1 teaspoon of salt & pepper and lightly coat with spray oil.
10. Cook for 12 minutes at 160°C in your Cair fryer.
11. Turn up to 200°C for around 6-8 minutes. Check after 5 minutes as depending on size they can cook quickly.

Nutritional Value (Amount per Serving):

Calories: 389; Fat: 5.01; Carb: 81.9; Protein: 5.4

Chapter 3: Vegetables

Air Fryer Parsnips

Prep Time: 5 Minutes
Cook Time: 15 Minutes   Serves: 4

Ingredients:

- 4 medium parsnips
- 1 tbsp oil
- Salt and pepper to taste

Directions:

1. Top and tail the parsnips. Optionally peel the parsnips.
2. Drizzle oil over the parsnips and toss until they are covered.
3. Season with salt and pepper according to taste.
4. Transfer the parsnips to the air fryer basket.
5. Set the temperature to 200°C and air fry for 15 minutes.
6. Shake the air fryer basket at the halfway mark.
7. The parsnips will be soft in the middle and golden brown on the outside when they are ready, if necessary, air fry for longer.

Nutritional Value (Amount per Serving):

Calories: 107; Fat: 3.88; Carb: 16.49; Protein: 3.31

Air Fryer Brussel Sprouts

Prep Time: 10 Minutes
Cook Time: 15 Minutes   Serves: 4

Ingredients:

- 400g Brussel sprouts, halved
- 200g bacon lardons
- 1/2 tsp garlic granules
- 2 tbsp parmesan cheese (optional)
- Salt and pepper to season

Directions:

1. Slice the Brussel sprouts in half and place them in a bowl.
2. Sprinkle the garlic granules over them and optionally salt and pepper. Toss

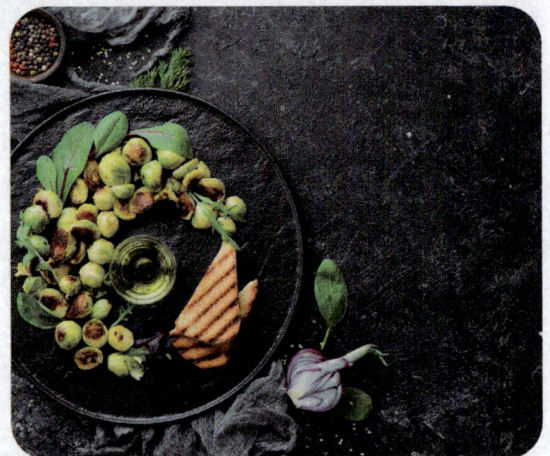

the sprouts about so that they all get covered.

3. Add the bacon lardons and mix in.

4. Transfer to the air fryer basket and cook at 180°C for 15 to 20 minutes. Check on them halfway through and give them a shake. They are ready when they are soft on the inside and browned on the outside.

5. Optionally sprinkle with cheese, either 1 minute before the end of the cooking time or while they are still hot so that the cheese can melt a little bit.

Nutritional Value (Amount per Serving):

Calories: 214; Fat: 15.78; Carb: 13.64; Protein: 9.68

Air Fryer Broccoli

Prep Time: 5 Minutes
Cook Time: 10 Minutes   Serves:

Ingredients:

- 1 head of broccoli
- 2 tsp garlic powder
- 2 tsp onion powder
- 1 - 2 tbsp olive oil
- Parmesan cheese (optional)

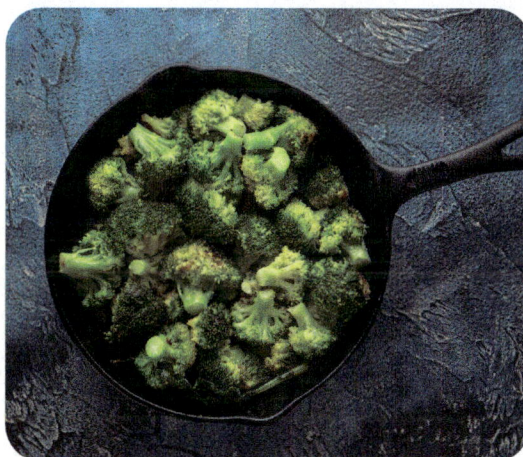

Directions:

1. Preheat the air fryer to 190°C.

2. Prepare the broccoli by breaking up the florets into evenly sized pieces. If necessary use a sharp knife to slice up.

3. In a bowl mix the olive oil and seasoning and stir.

4. Add the sliced broccoli to the bowl and roll it about to roughly coat it.

5. Place the broccoli in the air fryer basket. Depending on the size of the air fryer you might need to cook it in batches.

6. Cook for 10 to 15 minutes, checking on it at 5 minutes to give it a shake. Depending on the size of the broccoli it might cook in more or less time so keep an eye on it. The broccoli is ready when it is tender and starting to brown and crisp up.

7. Optionally sprinkle with parmesan cheese before serving.

Nutritional Value (Amount per Serving):

Calories: 342; Fat: 28.44; Carb: 13.07; Protein: 10.5

Air Fryer Garlic And Herb Potatoes

Prep Time: 5 Minutes
Cook Time: 20 Minutes   Serves:

Ingredients:

- 1kg new potatoes
- 2-3 sprigs rosemary
- Handful fresh parsley
- 2 tbsp garlic granules/powder
- 2 tsp salt
- 2 tbsp of olive oil

Directions:

1. Chop the potatoes into even-sized chunks, halving the medium ones and quartering the large ones.
2. Finely chop the parsley and the rosemary (leaves only).
3. Place the potatoes in a large bowl, and sprinkle over the chopped herbs, the garlic granules and salt. Drizzle over with olive oil and mix until all potatoes are well-coated.
4. Cook in air fryer at 200°C for 20 minutes, shaking after 10 minutes. If you have a smaller air fryer, you may have to cook for longer or in 2 small batches.

Nutritional Value (Amount per Serving):

Calories: 1077; Fat: 28.2; Carb: 189.39; Protein: 23.52

Air Fryer Hasselback Potatoes

Prep Time: 5 Minutes
Cook Time: 30 Minutes   Serves: 4

Ingredients:

- 4 medium potatoes
- Salt and pepper
- Spray oil
- Garlic butter – to make this you'll need butter

Directions:

1. Slice your potatoes 3/4 of the way through (see near the top of this post for my method). Be sure to use a sharp knife and do not slice all the way through the potato.
2. Use spray oil on the potatoes.
3. Season with salt and pepper.
4. Brush each of the slices on both sides using melted garlic butter.
5. Cook at 180°C for 15 minutes.
6. Remove using tongs. Place on to a chopping board.
7. Completely baste/brush all of the slices again.
8. Cook at 180°C for another 10 minutes.
9. Brush/baste the potatoes again.
10. Cook at 180°C for another 5-10 minutes, depending on the size.

Nutritional Value (Amount per Serving):

Calories: 301; Fat: 1.7; Carb: 65.58; Protein: 7.62

Air Fryer Parsnips Recipe (Honey Glazed)

Prep Time: 5 Minutes
Cook Time: 18 Minutes   Serves: 2

Ingredients:

- 250 g parsnips
- 15 ml honey
- Salt & pepper to taste

Directions:

1. Wash and peel your parsnips.
2. Slice them lengthways into 4 or 6 pieces, depending on the size and length of parsnips.
3. Drizzle over the honey.
4. Add your seasoning.
5. Place your honey glazed air fryer parsnips in your air fryer.
6. Cook at 200°C for approximately 18 minutes. Start checking from 15 minutes onwards.

Nutritional Value (Amount per Serving):

Calories: 749; Fat: 0.42; Carb: 199.84; Protein: 2.59

Air Fryer Roasted Tomatoes

Prep Time: 2 Minutes
Cook Time: 20 Minutes   Serves: 4

Ingredients:

- 8 tomatoes
- 15 ml vegetable oil
- 4 cloves of garlic
- 10 sprigs of thyme
- 1 sprig of rosemary
- Generous pinch of salt and pepper

Directions:

1. Wash your tomatoes. Dry thoroughly.
2. Place in a bowl with the vegetable oil and garlic cloves.
3. Mix well until all tomatoes are coated.
4. Add the herbs and salt and pepper.
5. Cook at 200°C for 20 minutes. Check at the 10 minute mark and shake gently if needed, although you shouldn't need to!

Nutritional Value (Amount per Serving):

Calories: 937; Fat: 102.79; Carb: 12.29; Protein: 2.73

Slow Cooker Leek And Potato Soup

Prep Time: 20 Minutes
Cook Time: 6 Hours   Serves: 4-6

Ingredients:

- 8 potatoes, chopped
- 3 leeks, chopped
- 1 onion, chopped
- 2 tbsp. butter
- 2 x vegetable stock pots/cubes
- 1 litre boiling water
- Seasoning - salt/celery salt/black pepper
- Optional: single cream, cooked bacon and/or Stilton cheese

Directions:

1. Peel and chop potatoes to equal sizes and add to the cooker.
2. Add leeks, onions and butter.
3. Dilute 2 stock cubes in 1 litre of boiling water.
4. Add stock to the slow cooker so that it just covers the ingredients. Add any preferred seasoning and stir everything together.
5. Set off on high for 4 hours, or low for 6 - 8 hours.
6. When finished - the ingredients should be soft - blend with a stick blender, or, transfer to a large blender. If you prefer a chunkier consistency, you might choose just to pulse or mash the soup with a potato masher.

Nutritional Value (Amount per Serving):

Calories: 620; Fat: 11.2; Carb: 118.97; Protein: 14.8

Chapter 4: Meats

Pressure Cooker Ox Cheek Carrots In Red Wine

Prep Time: 40 Minutes
Cook Time: 1 Hour   Serves: 4

Ingredients:

- 1 kg ox cheeks, in 4 pieces
- 500ml red wine
- 5 bay leaves
- small bunch of thyme
- 1 small star anise
- 1 whole clove
- 2 tbsp vegetable oil
- 6 carrots, 2 roughly chopped, 4 left whole
- 1 large onion, roughly chopped
- 2 celery sticks, roughly chopped
- 2 garlic cloves, chopped
- 500ml beef stock
- creamy mash, to serve

Directions:

1. Up to two days before you want to serve or at least 1 hr before, put the ox cheeks in a large bowl. Pour over the wine and add the herbs, the star anise, clove and a good grinding of black pepper. Cover and chill.
2. Remove the ox cheeks from the wine, reserving the wine. Pat dry using kitchen paper and season. Heat the oil in the multi-cooker, then brown the ox cheeks well on all sides over a medium-high heat. Remove to a plate. Add the carrots, onion, celery and garlic and cook for 10 minutes until browned.
3. Return the ox cheeks to the pan and pour over the reserved wine and any herbs still in it. Bring to the boil and skim off any foam that rises to the surface, then pour in the pot. Bring everything to a simmer, cover and bring up to high pressure. Cook for 45 Minutes, then release the pressure. Take the lid off, add the whole carrots, cover again with the lid, bring back up to high pressure and cook for another 15 minutes, or until the ox cheeks are tender and the carrots are cooked through. Once cooked, leave the beef to rest in the liquid until cool – this will deepen the flavour. Will keep chilled

for a day. Leave to cool completely first.

4. Lift the ox cheeks and whole carrots out of the pan and into a bowl. Pass the cooking liquid through a fine sieve into a saucepan. Simmer over a medium heat for 15-20 minutes, or until reduced to a rich sauce. Season and return the ox cheeks and carrots to the sauce to warm through. Serve the ox cheeks with the carrots and some mash.

Nutritional Value (Amount per Serving):

Calories: 1120; Fat: 17.19; Carb: 232.1; Protein: 7.18

Pressure Cooker Beef Curry

Prep Time: 10 Minutes
Cook Time: 40 Minutes - 50 Minutes
  Serves: 4

Ingredients:

- 2 tbsp sunflower oil
- 500g beef, stewing or braising steak
- 1 tbsp butter
- 1 large onion, chopped
- 2 garlic cloves, crushed
- 1 thumb-sized piece ginger, finely grated
- ¼ tsp hot chilli powder
- 1 tsp turmeric
- 2 tsp ground coriander
- 3 cardamom pods, crushed
- 400g can chopped tomatoes
- ½ small bunch of coriander, roughly chopped
- naan bread or rice, to serve
- 500ml beef stock
- 1 tsp caster sugar
- 2 tsp garam masala
- 2 tbsp double cream (optional)

Directions:

1. Heat 1 tbsp of the oil in the multi-cooker. Season the beef and fry in batches for 5-8 minutes, turning occasionally until evenly browned. Set aside on a plate.
2. Heat the remaining oil and butter in the pan and fry the onion gently for 10 minutes or until golden brown and caramelised. Add the garlic, ginger, chilli, turmeric, coriander and cardamom and fry for 2 minutes. Stir in the

beef and cook for 1 min to coat the beef in the spices.

3. Tip in the tomatoes, stock and sugar and bring to a simmer. Lock the lid onto the cooker and bring up to high pressure. Cook for 15 minutes, then turn off the heat and let the pressure drop naturally. Give everything a good stir and add more water if the sauce is already thick.

4. Lock the lid back in place and give it another 10 minutes, then let the pressure drop naturally. Check the meat is tender – depending on the cut it might need 5 minutes more.

5. Take it off the heat, stir through the garam masala and cream, if you like. Season to taste. Scatter over the coriander and serve with naan bread or rice.

Nutritional Value (Amount per Serving):

Calories: 465; Fat: 23.1; Carb: 34.14; Protein: 32.76

Slow Cooker Meatballs

Prep Time: 5 Minutes
Cook Time: 5 Hours   Serves: 4

Ingredients:

- 24 meatballs (approx - either pre-prepared or homemade)
- 1tbsp dried Italian herbs
- 2 x 400g tomato passata or tinned tomatoes
- 1tbsp tomato puree
- 1 onion
- 2 cloves garlic
- Basil leaves (optional, for garnish)

Directions:

1. Gently sear the meatballs before adding them to the multi-cooker - this is optional but I prefer to seal the meat to help lock in the juices as well as reduce the risk of the meatballs falling apart in the slow cooker.

2. Add the sauce ingredients straight to the multi-cooker and mix together.

3. Transfer the meatballs to the multi-cooker so that they are submerged in the sauce.

4. Set off on low for 4 to 5 hours.

5. Remove the lid and gently stir the sauce around - take care not to break up

the meatballs.
6. Serve over cooked spaghetti and sprinkle with grated cheese and fresh basil leaves.

Nutritional Value (Amount per Serving):

Calories: 122; Fat: 4.92; Carb: 7.83; Protein: 11.85

Slow Cooker BBQ Pork Ribs

Prep Time: 10 Minutes
Cook Time: 8 Hours   Serves:

Ingredients:

- 1 kg pork ribs
- 300ml barbecue sauce
- 1 tbsp Worcestershire sauce
- 3 cloves garlic, crushed
- 1 tbsp smoked paprika

Directions:

1. In a bowl, mix together the barbecue sauce, Worcestershire sauce, crushed garlic and smoked paprika.
2. Place the pork ribs directly into the slow cooker.
3. Pour three-quarters of the sauce over the pork ribs, reserving the remaining quarter to use later.
4. Place the lid on the cooker and set off on low for 7 to 8 hours, or high for 3 to 4 hours.
5. Carefully remove the pork ribs from the cooker, taking care not to let the soft meat fall apart. Place them in a baking tray.
6. Scoop out a few spoonfuls of the liquid left in the cooker and stir it in with the reserved BBQ sauce from step 3.
7. Drizzle this sauce over the pork ribs and grill for 5 to 10 minutes or until they start to crisp up.

Nutritional Value (Amount per Serving):

Calories: 856; Fat: 28.69; Carb: 28.32; Protein: 113.46

Slow Cooker BBQ Ribs

Prep Time: 10 Minutes
Cook Time: 4 Hours   Serves: 3

Ingredients:

- 500 g ribs I used pork
- 200 ml BBQ sauce
- 1 tsp brown sugar
- 1/2 tsp garlic puree
- Splash Worcestershire sauce
- 1/2 tsp cayenne pepper

Directions:

1. Remove the membrane from your ribs if you're using a full rack of ribs.
2. Combine all of your ingredients apart from the ribs.
3. Keep back about 1/3 of the liquid.
4. Spread over all of the ribs ensuring even coverage the best you can.
5. Place into your multi-cooker.
6. Cook on high for 4 hours or low for 8 hours. The longer you cook them the more tender they will be!
7. Optional: Pour over the last 1/3 of the liquid at the end of cooking and grill for a couple of minutes.
8. Alternatively, use the sauce as a dipping sauce by warming it through before serving.

Nutritional Value (Amount per Serving):

Calories: 260; Fat: 9.57; Carb: 6.37; Protein: 35.69

Air Fryer Sausages

Prep Time: 3 Minutes
Cook Time: 10 Minutes   Serves: 8

Ingredients:

- 8 sausages

Directions:

1. Preheat the air fryer to 180°C.
2. Pierce each sausage with a knife or fork.
3. Lay sausages in the basket.
4. Cook for 10 minutes, checking on them and turning them over after 5 minutes.

Nutritional Value (Amount per Serving):

Calories: 73; Fat: 5.15; Carb: 2.79; Protein: 5.25

Air Fryer Meatballs

Prep Time: 10 Minutes
Cook Time: 7 Minutes   Serves:

Ingredients:

- 500g lean beef mince
- 1 clove garlic, crushed
- 1 tsp dried mixed herbs
- 1 egg
- 1tbsp breadcrumbs, (optional)

Directions:

1. Mix all ingredients together until well combined.
2. Using your hands, form small round balls (this recipe makes about 16, depending on size of meatballs)
3. Place meatballs in air fryer and cook at 180°C for 7 minutes. Check half way through and turn over if necessary.
4. If you want to add a sauce, once the meatballs are cooked transfer them to an ovenproof dish/pan that will fit in the Air fryer. Pour your choice of tomato sauce on top and place container in Air fryer tray. Cook at 180°C for about 6-8 minutes, or until the sauce is warmed through.
5. Serve with spaghetti and melted cheese.

Nutritional Value (Amount per Serving):

Calories: 799; Fat: 38.2; Carb: 2.02; Protein: 111.76

Air Fryer Bacon

Prep Time: 2 Minutes
Cook Time: 10 Minutes   Serves: 2

Ingredients:

- 2 rashers smoked bacon
- Alternatively
- 2 rashers streaky bacon

Directions:

1. Preheat your air fryer to 200°C for a couple of minutes.
2. Place your bacon of choice in a single layer in your basket. It is ok if it overlaps slightly, or the edges fold over slightly.
3. You may need to repeat the cooking a couple of times if you have a lot of bacon, or a smaller air fryer basket (like I currently do!).
4. Cooking times are as follows:
5. Smoked streaky bacon rashers – 200°C– 11 minutes.
6. Smoked bacon rashers – 200°C – 10 minutes.
7. Smoked bacon medallions – 200°C – 8 minutes.

Nutritional Value (Amount per Serving):

Calories: 1456; Fat: 138.63; Carb: 29.68; Protein: 50.15

Chapter 5: Poultry

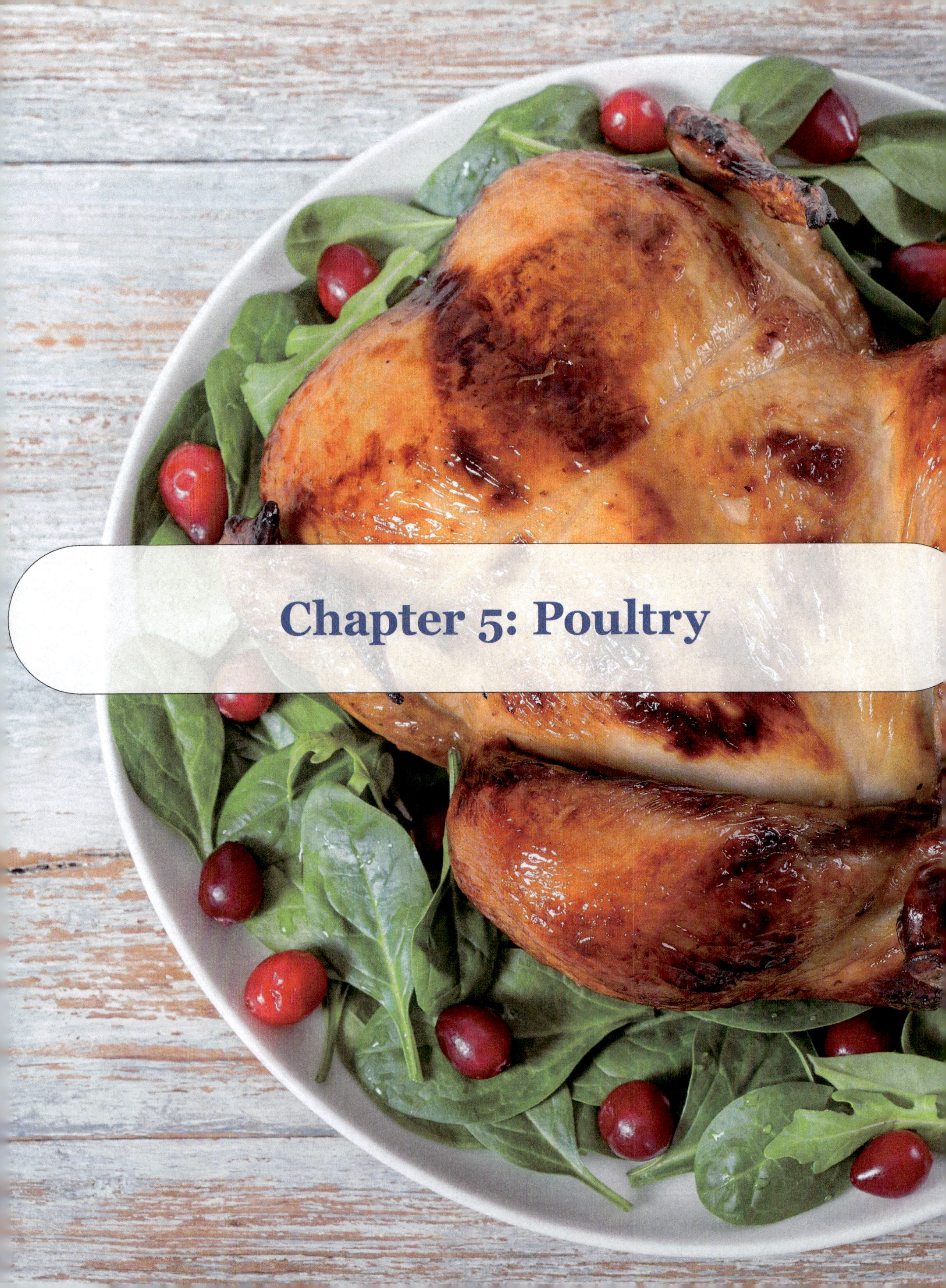

20 Minutes Whole Chicken

Prep Time: 10 Minutes
Cook Time: 20 Minutes   Serves: 4

Ingredients:

- or The Chicken
- 1 whole chicken see above for cooking times
- 1 onion cut into slices
- 1 potato peeled and sliced
- 1 carrot peeled and sliced
- 1 stick celery chopped roughly
- 3 cloves garlic peeled
- low calorie cooking spray
- or The Seasoning
- 1 tbsp thyme
- 2 tbsp paprika
- the zest of 1 lemon reserve the juice for the stock
- sea salt
- freshly ground black pepper
- or The Stock
- the juice of 1 lemon use the zest for the rub
- 1 chicken stock cube made up with 400ml of boiling water

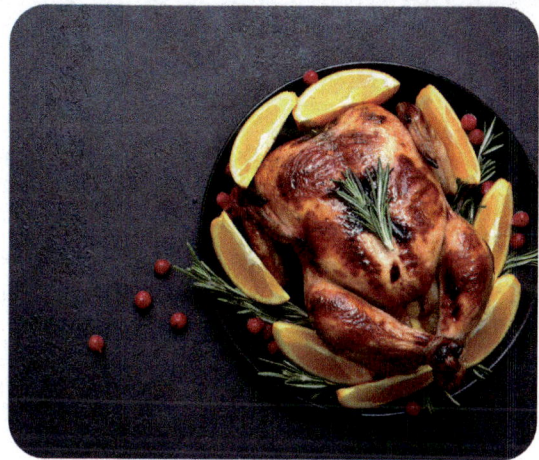

Directions:

1. Mix all the seasoning ingredients together, then rub all over the chicken. Lift the skin up on the breast and rub some seasoning between the skin and the breast.
2. Put left over lemon (after zesting and squeezing) in the cavity.
3. Put the multi-cooker into Sauté, spray with some low calorie cooking spray, then brown the chicken on all sides. A couple of minutes on each side should be enough to colour it.
4. Take the chicken out and turn off the cooker.
5. Add a bit of the stock to the pot, and make sure to scrape any bits that may be stuck to the bottom of the pot.

6. To add flavour to the chicken, place the garlic, onion, potato, celery and carrots on the bottom - pour in the stock and lemon juice.
1. Place the chicken on top.
2. Put the lid on the cooker with the valve set to sealing - cook on Manual for 20 minutes for a small chicken, 25 minutes for a medium, 30 minutes for a large.
3. Let the pressure release naturally (aka NPR) then take out the chicken and let rest for 5 minutes before taking the skin off. Discard the cooked vegetables.
4. If you wish to use the juice that comes from the chicken, make sure to skim off the fat or use a fat separator and blitz to make a jus. Or, if you prefer a thicker sauce, blitz the juice with the discarded, cooked vegetables.

Nutritional Value (Amount per Serving):

Calories: 604; Fat: 24.1; Carb: 22.47; Protein: 71.71

Air Fryer Chicken Thighs

Prep Time: 5 Minutes
Cook Time: 25 Minutes   Serves:

Ingredients:

- 1kg chicken thighs
- 2 tsp Season All

Directions:

1. Preheat air fryer to 200°C.
2. Pat chicken thighs dry with some kitchen paper before seasoning.
3. Put seasoned chicken thighs in the hot air fryer. Depending on the size of your air fryer you may need to do this in batches, or, if you can, use a trivet or shelf.
4. Cook for 10 minutes before turning the thighs over. Cook for a further 10 minutes. They should be crispy and cooked through - if they are not, return them to the air fryer for a further 5 minutes, or until they are cooked. The internal temperature should be 75°C.
5. Serve with your favourite side dish!

Nutritional Value (Amount per Serving):

Calories: 3358; Fat: 224.5; Carb: 145.61; Protein: 186.86

Air Fryer Piri Piri Chicken Legs

Prep Time: 5 Minutes
Cook Time: 22 Minutes   Serves: 4

Ingredients:

- 4 chicken legs
- 2 tsp Piri Piri spice mix
- 120g Piri Piri marinade sauce (approx)

Directions:

1. Add the spice mix and sauce to the raw chicken legs. Leave them to marinate for around 30 minutes.
2. Transfer to the air fryer basket and cook at 190°C for 22 minutes.
3. Turn the chicken legs at the halfway mark.
4. The chicken legs are ready when the juices run clear and the internal temperature is 75°C–use a meat thermometer if necessary.

Nutritional Value (Amount per Serving):

Calories: 345; Fat: 11.19; Carb: 4.87; Protein: 52.55

Air Fryer Chicken Breasts

Prep Time: 10 Minutes
Cook Time: 20 Minutes   Serves: 4

Ingredients:

- 1 chicken breast (increase accordingly)
- 1/2 tbsp olive oil
- 1/2 tsp salt
- 1/2 tsp pepper
- 1/2 tsp garlic powder (or seasoning of your choice)

Directions:

1. Preheat the air fryer at 180°C.
2. Brush or spray each chicken breast with oil.
3. Season one side (the smooth side) of each chicken breast.
4. Place each chicken breast (smooth side down) in the air fryer basket.

Season the other side.

5. Set the timer for 10 minutes.
6. After 10 minutes turn the chicken breasts over to allow them to cook on both sides.
7. Check the chicken is cooked all the way through - use a meat thermometer if necessary.
8. Leave the chicken to rest for 5 minutes before serving or slicing.

Nutritional Value (Amount per Serving):

Calories: 143; Fat: 8.42; Carb: 0.82; Protein: 15.29

Air Fryer Chicken Wings

Prep Time: 5 Minutes
Cook Time: 25 Minutes   Serves: 4

Ingredients:

- 1 kg chicken wings
- 1 tbsp olive oil
- ½ tsp garlic powder
- ½ tsp onion powder
- ½ tsp paprika
- ½ tsp salt
- ½ tsp black pepper

Directions:

1. Preheat the air fryer at 180°C.
2. Prepare the chicken wings by firstly patting them dry with some kitchen roll. The dryer the chicken wings are, the crispier they will come out.
3. Add the wings to a large bowl and cover with the olive oil, tossing them so that they are all covered as much as possible.
4. Add all the seasonings, coating all the wings.
5. Put the chicken wings in the air fryer. Depending on how many wings you are cooking, and the size of your air fryer, you might need to do them in batches. You can also use a rack in your air fryer to fit more in. The key thing is to make sure the wings are not touching each other so that they have room to crisp up.
6. Cook for 20 minutes, turning and shaking 2 or 3 times to ensure they cook evenly.
7. Increase the temperature to 200°C and cook for a further 5 minutes or until

the skin is crispy.

8.Serve with BBQ sauce, Hot Pepper Sauce, Buffalo Sauce

Nutritional Value (Amount per Serving):

Calories: 561; Fat: 35.11; Carb: 9.28; Protein: 49.35

Air Fryer Hunters Chicken

Prep Time: 5 Minutes
Cook Time: 25 Minutes   Serves: 2

Ingredients:

- 2 chicken breasts (1 chicken breast per person)
- 4 rashers of bacon (1 or 2 per chicken piece)
- 6 tbsp BBQ sauce
- 50g grated cheese (cheddar, mozzarella, gouda or parmesan)

Directions:

1.Place the chicken breasts in the air fryer basket at 190°C and set the timer for 10 minutes; if you have a small air fryer basket, you might only be able to fit two at a time. Turn the chicken at the 5-minute mark.
2.After 10 minutes of cooking time, using some tongs or a fork, remove the chicken breasts and wrap each one in one or two rashers of bacon. To keep the rashers in place, you can use a cocktail stick.
3.Return the bacon-wrapped chicken to the air fryer basket and cook for a further 10 minutes, again turning halfway.
4.At the end of the cooking time, open the air fryer basket and brush the BBQ sauce equally over each chicken breast.
5.Sprinkle the grated cheese over the top of the BBQ sauce.
6.Air fry for a further 2 to 3 minutes or until the cheese has melted and the BBQ sauce is hot.
7.Remove from the air fryer, and remove the cocktail sticks if you used them.
8.Check the chicken is cooked all the way through, either by cutting into one or using a meat thermometer.
9.Serve with your favourite side dish.

Nutritional Value (Amount per Serving):

Calories: 1803; Fat: 118.5; Carb: 3.96; Protein: 169.98

Air Fryer Cajun Chicken

Prep Time: 5 Minutes
Cook Time: 20 Minutes   Serves: 4

Ingredients:

- 640 g chicken mini fillets
- Cajun seasoning see my recipe

Directions:

1. Add your chicken to a bowl.
2. Add your cajun seasoning and rub all over the chicken fillets.
3. Lightly oil the air fryer basket (if desired – I use spray rapeseed oil)
4. Add your chicken mini fillets to the air fryer.
5. Cook on 200°C for 20 minutes, turning 10 minutes in.
6. If you overload the air fryer basket a little, like me, then you'll want to give these a shake a couple of times during the 20 minutes.
7. Check the temperature before serving. Chicken should be at least 74°C internally before serving.

Nutritional Value (Amount per Serving):

Calories: 462; Fat: 18.08; Carb: 51.76; Protein: 22.3

Chapter 6: Appetizers and Snacks

Air Fryer Burger

Prep Time: 5 Minutes
Cook Time: 8 Minutes   Serves: 2

Ingredients:

- 2 burger patties - fresh or frozen
- 1/2 onion, chopped
- 2 burger baps
- 2 slices cheese (optional)
- 2 lettuce leaves (optional)
- 1 tomato, sliced

Directions:

1. Lay the burger patties in the air fryer basket. If you want to cook the onion at the same time you can also add these now.
2. Set the air fryer off at 180°C for 8 minutes.
3. At the 4 minute mark, flip the burger over.
4. At the 8-minute mark check whether the burger is cooked through, the juices should run clear.
5. If you want to turn it into a cheeseburger, lay the slices of cheese over each burger. You can also lightly toast the burger baps at the same time by inserting a trivet and laying them on top of it.
6. Air fry for a further minute, or until the cheese has melted and the baps are lightly toasted.
7. Assemble the burgers in the baps with you choice of salad and sauces.

Nutritional Value (Amount per Serving):

Calories: 1177; Fat: 82.27; Carb: 13.89; Protein: 90.43

Air Fryer Sweet Potato Wedges

Prep Time: 10 Minutes
Cook Time: 20 Minutes   Serves: 4

Ingredients:

- 4 large sweet potatoes
- 1 tbsp oil (I used olive oil)
- 1 tsp smoked paprika
- 1 tsp garlic powder
- Salt and pepper according to taste

Directions:

1. Preheat the air fryer to 200°C.
2. Prepare the sweet potatoes by chopping off the ends and cleaning them. Slice them lengthwise into similar-sized wedges.
3. Drizzle with oil and add seasoning. Toss the sweet potato wedges in the oil and seasoning, ensuring they are all coated.
4. Transfer to the air fryer basket and set the timer for 20 minutes. Check on them at the halfway mark to shake them about.
5. After 20 minutes, they should be crispy on the outside and soft and fluffy on the inside. If they are not, return them to the air fryer and continue cooking, checking on them after 2 minutes.
6. Serve the sweet potato wedges as a side dish or with your favourite dip.

Nutritional Value (Amount per Serving):

Calories: 323; Fat: 3.83; Carb: 66.4; Protein: 7.89

Air Fryer Potato Slices

Prep Time: 5 Minutes
Cook Time: 18 Minutes   Serves: 4

Ingredients:

- 4 large potatoes
- 1 tbsp olive oil
- 1 tsp garlic granules
- 1 tsp dried mixed herbs
- 1/2 tsp salt

Directions:

1. Wash and cut the potatoes into 1/2 cm slices.
2. Put the sliced potatoes in a pot of water.
3. Once all the potatoes have been sliced, drain the water and pat the potatoes dry with kitchen paper or a clean kitchen towel.
4. Add the oil, garlic, herbs and salt to the dry sliced potatoes, tossing them about until they are all coated.
5. Transfer the sliced potatoes to the air fryer basket and cook at 200°C for 18 minutes, shaking halfway through. The potato slices should be crispy on the outside and soft on the inside. If they are not, return to the air fryer for a further two minutes.
6. Serve as a side dish or as a snack.

Nutritional Value (Amount per Serving):

Calories: 315; Fat: 3.71; Carb: 64.7; Protein: 7.5

Air Fryer Boiled Eggs

Prep Time: 1 Minute
Cook Time: 10 Minutes   Serves:

Ingredients:

- 4 eggs (cook as many as you need)

Directions:

1. Add room temperature eggs to the basket of your air fryer, and leave some space between them so that there is room for the hot air to circulate. Use a metal rack if needed to fit more in.
2. Set the air fryer temperature at 150°C. Cook according to how well done you want your eggs (starting at 8 minutes for runny, up to 12 minutes for hard boiled).
3. At the end of the cooking time remove from the air fryer basket and plunge into an ice bath or into a bowl of cold water – this will prevent the eggs from continuing to cook.
4. Once they have cooled down a little and can be handled, remove the shell

Nutritional Value (Amount per Serving):

Calories: 1086; Fat: 71.54; Carb: 81.36; Protein: 32.68

Ninja Foodi Roast Potatoes

Prep Time: 10 Minutes
Cook Time: 27 Minutes   Serves: 4

Ingredients:

- 1kg Maris Pipers or King Edwards
- 500ml boiling water
- 1tbsp olive oil – or oil/fat of your choice
- Salt and pepper
- Optional seasoning – rosemary, sage, thyme and or garlic

Directions:

1. Peel and quarter the potatoes. Rinse them under some water before placing in the air fryer basket of the Ninja Foodi.
2. Pour 500ml of boiling water in the cooking pot of the Ninja Foodi before placing the basket inside.
3. Place the pressure cooker lid on the Ninja Foodi and select high pressure for 2 minutes. Remember to check the valve is in the seal position.
4. When the pressure cooker has finished, perform a quick release before carefully removing the lid.
5. Take the basket with the potatoes in them out of the Ninja Foodi, taking care not to burn your hands.
6. Give the potatoes a gentle shake to fluff them up - this will help to crisp them up.
7. Pour the water from the Ninja Foodi pot.
8. Drizzle the oil over the potatoes, you might need to use a brush to make sure they are all covered. You may prefer to transfer the potatoes to a larger bowl if you find there is not enough space to oil them up in the basket.
9. Season with your choice of herbs, or just with salt and pepper if preferred.
10. Return the seasoned potatoes to the Ninja Foodi cooking pot (in the basket) and close the lid.
11. Select the air fryer function and cook at 200°C for 25 minutes, checking on them 3 or 4 times and turning to make sure they are evenly crisped up.

Nutritional Value (Amount per Serving):

Calories: 2689; Fat: 53.64; Carb: 414.72; Protein: 136.69

Air Fryer Halloumi

Prep Time: 2 Minutes
Cook Time: 8 Minutes   Serves: 8

Ingredients:

- 225g halloumi
- 1 tbsp olive oil
- 1/2 tsp dried thyme (optional)

Directions:

1. Preheat the air fryer to 200°C.
2. Slice halloumi and brush with oil on both sides. Sprinkle with seasoning if using.
3. Transfer halloumi slices to the air fryer basket and air fry for 8 to 10 minutes, turning over halfway.
4. The halloumi is ready when it has softened and is beginning to turn brown around the edges.

Nutritional Value (Amount per Serving):

Calories: 97; Fat: 7.66; Carb: 2.47; Protein: 4.62

Air Fryer Carrot Cake

Prep Time: 10 Minutes
Cook Time: 25 Minutes   Serves: 1

Ingredients:

- 140g Soft brown sugar
- 2 eggs, beaten
- 140g butter
- 1 orange, zest & juice
- 200g self-raising flour
- 1tsp ground cinnamon
- 175g grated carrot, (approx 2 medium carrots)
- 60g sultanas

Directions:

1. Preheat air fryer to 175°C.

2. In a bowl, cream together the butter and sugar.
3. Slowly add the beaten eggs.
4. Fold in the flour, a little bit at a time, mixing it as you go. Add the orange juice and zest, grated carrots and sultanas. Gently mix all the ingredients together.
5. Grease the baking tin and pour the mixture in.
6. Place baking tin in the air fryer basket and cook for 25-30 minutes. Check and see if the cake has cooked - use a cocktail stick or metal skewer to poke in the middle. If it comes out wet then cook it for a little longer.
7. Remove the baking tin from the air fryer basket and allow to cool for 10 minutes before removing from the tin.

Nutritional Value (Amount per Serving):

Calories: 2647; Fat: 135.17; Carb: 314.17; Protein: 41.41

Air Fryer Chicken Nuggets

Prep Time: 10 Minutes
Cook Time: 8 Minutes   Serves: 4

Ingredients:

- 3-4 boneless chicken breasts
- 2 eggs, beaten
- 100g breadcrumbs, (approx)
- Seasoning of your choice, eg; 1tsp smoked paprika, 1tsp garlic granules, 1/2 tsp salt, 1/2 tsp pepper.

Directions:

1. Cut chicken breasts up into small chicken nugget-sized chunks.
2. Set up a chicken nugget breading station of three bowls. Add the beaten egg to one bowl, mix the seasoning with the breadcrumbs, add to a different bowl, and put the raw chicken pieces in another bowl.
3. Using kitchen tongs, dip the chicken in the beaten egg, then roll it in the seasoned breadcrumbs. Place in air fryer basket.
4. Repeat with each piece of chicken. Depending on the size of your air fryer, you may need to cook in 2 separate batches.
5. Cook at 200°C for 8 to 10 minutes. Check the chicken nuggets are cooked through before serving.

Nutritional Value (Amount per Serving):

Calories: 767; Fat: 40.24; Carb: 1.57; Protein: 94.01

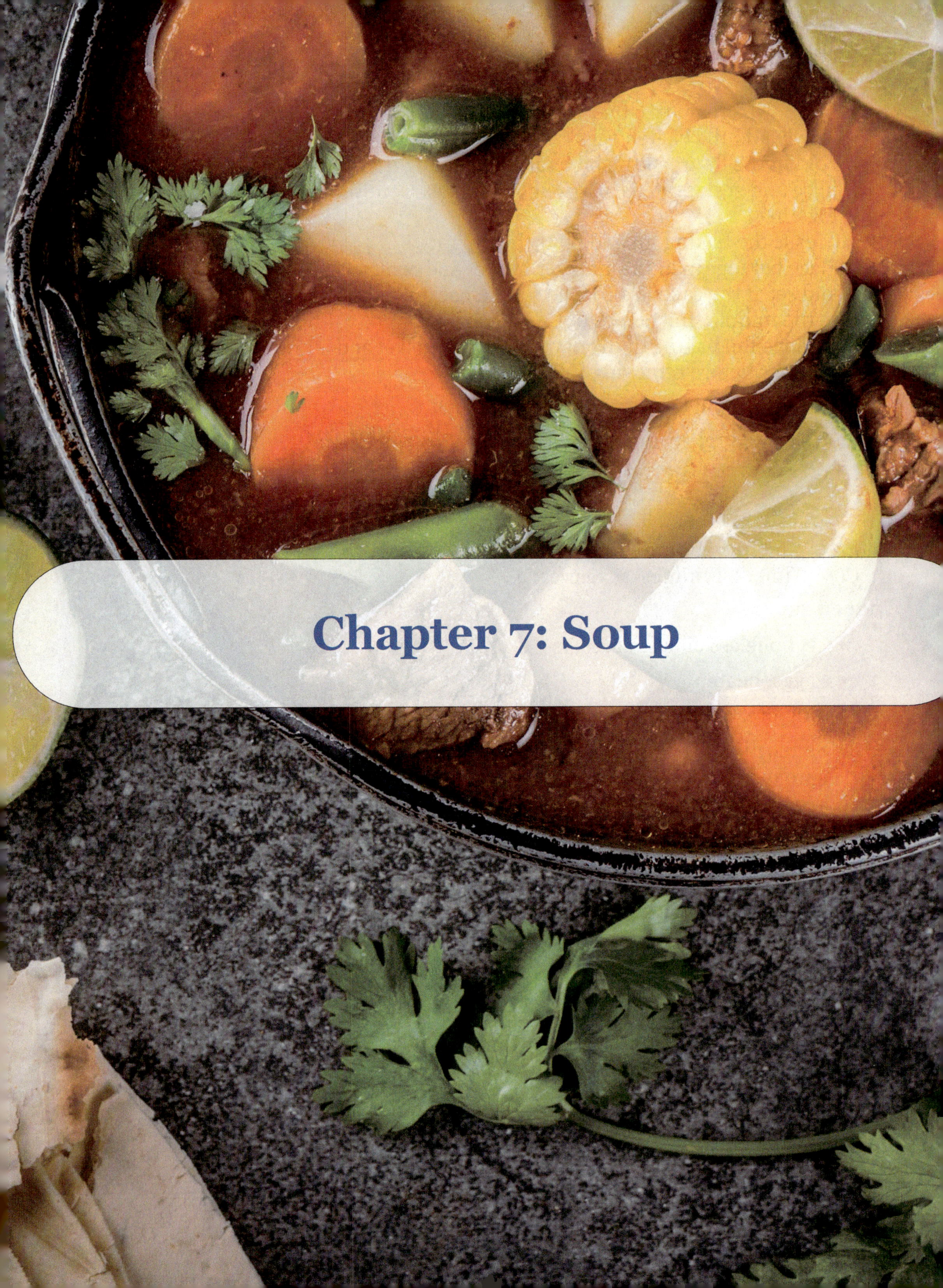

Chapter 7: Soup

Slow Cooker Porridge

Prep Time: 5 Minutes
Cook Time: 6 Hours   Serves: 4

Ingredients:

- 200g jumbo oats
- 800ml milk or water (or a combination of both)
- Salt (optional)
- Cinnamon (optional)

Directions:

1. Mix oats and liquid together, either directly in the multi-cooker (grease the bowl first with a little butter or oil), or in a large casserole dish and place that in the slow cooker. If you are using a bowl within the slow cooker bowl, you can add some water around it too.
2. If you are adding salt, cinnamon or other seasoning, stir this in too.
3. Cook on low for between 2 and 6 hours. Use a timer or keep warm function if needed.
4. Stir the porridge before serving with your favourite toppings on top.

Nutritional Value (Amount per Serving):

Calories: 356; Fat: 13.12; Carb: 65.57; Protein: 12.92

Slow Cooker Minestrone Soup

Prep Time: 10 Minutes
Cook Time: 4 Hours   Serves: 6

Ingredients:

- 2 onions, chopped
- 2 cloves garlic, crushed
- 3 rashers smokey bacon, chopped (optional)
- 2 small courgettes, chopped
- 3 celery sticks, chopped
- 3 carrots, chopped
- 2 tins x 400g tomatoes

- ½ tsp dried oregano
- 2 bay leaves
- 1 litre of chicken or vegetable stock (from 2 stock pots/cubes)
- 100g dried soup pasta
- Large handful of spinach
- Salt and pepper to season

Directions:

1. Optionally saute the onions, garlic and bacon in a little oil. If you choose to do this step you can also saute the courgettes, celery and carrots.
2. Add everything to the cooker apart from the pasta and spinach.
3. Place the lid on and cook on low for 6 to 8 hours, or high for 3 to 4 hours.
4. Remove the lid and add the spinach and pasta. Cook for a further 20 to 30 minutes, or until the pasta is soft.
5. When finished, gently stir, season some more if required.
6. Serve with grated cheese (parmesan is a good choice) and crusty bread.

Nutritional Value (Amount per Serving):

Calories: 866; Fat: 73.45; Carb: 25.14; Protein: 39.48

Slow Cooker Chocolate Fudge

Prep Time: 5 Minutes
Cook Time: 1 Hour 30 Minutes   Serves: 30

Ingredients:

- 2 tbsp vanilla essence
- 2 tbsp butter
- 397 g condensed milk, (1 tin)
- 350 g milk chocolate

Directions:

1. Break up all the chocolate into squares and add to the cooker.
2. Add the other ingredients.
3. Switch your cooker on low. Leave the lid off.
4. Cook for around 90 minutes, stirring every 15 minutes with a wooden spoon.
5. Pour the mixture into a lined baking tin (I used 20cm) and allow to cool.
6. Transfer to the fridge to set (at least 3 hours).

7. Remove from fridge and chop up into chunks.

Nutritional Value (Amount per Serving):

Calories: 29; Fat: 1.66; Carb: 2.27; Protein: 0.84

Slow Cooker Dhal Soup

Prep Time: 20 Minutes
Cook Time: 8 Hours   Serves: 4

Ingredients:

- 1 red onion, finely diced
- 2 garlic cloves, crushed
- 5cm ginger, grated
- 500g butternut squash, peeled and cut into bite-size pieces
- 2 tsp ground cumin
- 1 tsp each turmeric and ground coriander
- 1 tsp chilli flakes (optional)
- 250g dried red lentils
- 2 x 200ml can Co-op light coconut milk
- 1 vegetable stock cube
- Fresh coriander, finely chopped chilli and toasted flatbreads, to serve

Directions:

1. In the multi-cooker, combine the onion, garlic, ginger, butternut squash and spices.
2. Stir in the lentils and coconut milk, then fill the empty can with water and add, along with the stock cube.
3. Cook on low for 8 hours.
4. Mash the butternut lightly with the back of a wooden spoon, leaving some pieces whole.
5. Garnish with the coriander and chilli and serve with the toasted flatbreads.

Nutritional Value (Amount per Serving):

Calories: 318; Fat: 3.63; Carb: 58.7; Protein: 16.96

Crock-Pot Slow Cooker Spicy Pumpkin And Butter

Prep Time: 10-15 Minutes
Cook Time: 5 Hours   Serves: 1

Ingredients:

- 1 medium sized pumpkin, peeled, seeds removed and cut into 1″ chunks
- 1 potato, peeled and cut into small chunks
- 2 white onions, peeled and cut into chunks
- 4 cloves garlic, chopped
- 450ml vegetable stock
- ½ tsp dried chilli flakes
- ½ tsp ground ginger
- ½ tsp ground nutmeg
- 1 tsp ground cumin
- 1 tsp ground cinnamon
- salt & freshly ground black pepper
- 2 x 400g cans butter beans, drained and rinsed
- milk or cream, to serve (optional)
- toasted pumpkin seeds, to serve (optional)

Directions:

1. Turn your multi-cooker to high.
2. Place all of the prepared vegetables and garlic into the pot.
3. Pour over the stock.
4. Sprinkle over the chilli flakes and spices and give everything a toss with a large spoon to coat everything.
5. Cook for 4 hours and after this time, puree in the pot with a hand-held immersion blender.
6. Taste and season with salt and freshly ground black pepper if you wish.
7. Stir in the butter beans and cook for a further hour.
8. To serve, pour into bowls, drizzle with a little milk or cream and sprinkle with the pumpkin seeds.

Nutritional Value (Amount per Serving):

Calories: 932; Fat: 89.3; Carb: 23.2; Protein: 16.12

Slow Cooker Crockpot Chicken Enchilada Soup

Prep Time: 20 Minutes
Cook Time: 4 Hours   Serves: 6

Ingredients:

- 0.33 floz olive oil
- 80 g onion chopped
- 3 garlic minced
- 23.84 floz chicken broth
- 226.8 g tomato sauce
- 0.17 floz chipotle chile in adobo sauce
- 4 g cilantro chopped
- 425.24 g black beans rinsed
- 411.07 g petite diced tomatoes
- 330 g frozen corn
- 4.93 g cumin
- 2.46 g dried oregano
- 0.45 kg chicken breast
- 0.25 scallions chopped
- 84.75 g cheddar cheese

Directions:

1. Heat oil and add in onions and garlic, saute.
2. Add in chicken broth, tomato sauce, chipotle adobo sauce, bring to boil.
3. Add in cilantro, pour into crock pot carefully.
4. Add in beans, diced tomatoes, corn, cumin, oregano, and stir.
5. Add in chicken.
6. Cook on low for 4-6 hours, shred chicken.
7. Serve with sour cream, cheddar cheese, scallions and cilantro.

Nutritional Value (Amount per Serving):

Calories: 496; Fat: 6.32; Carb: 74.76; Protein: 36.15

Slow Cooker Crock Pot Thai Coconut Chicken Soup

Prep Time: 10 Minutes
Cook Time: 4 Hours   Serves: 8

Ingredients:

- 565 g Chicken cooked, diced
- 2.03 floz Coconut Cream
- 39.74 floz Chicken or vegetable broth
- 2 Carrots medium, peeled and diced
- 0.5 Sweet pepper any color
- 9.86 g Ginger ground
- 4.93 g Garlic minced
- 0.75 floz Fish sauce optional
- 2.46 g Sugar
- Lime juice As desired
- Cilantro As desired

Directions:

1. Mix all ingredients except for the coconut cream in the slow cooker pot. Cook on low for 4 – 5 hours or high for 2 – 3 hours.
2. In the last ½ hour of cooking, add the coconut cream and let it mix in with the soup. Garnish with a sprinkling of cilantro if you like.

Nutritional Value (Amount per Serving):

Calories: 367; Fat: 31.88; Carb: 4.32; Protein: 15.36

Slow Cooker Mulled Cider

Prep Time: 5 Minutes
Cook Time: 1 Hour   Serves: 10

Ingredients:

- 1.5 litres dry cider
- 500ml apple juice
- 75g light brown soft sugar
- 1 orange, sliced
- ½ lemon, zest pared into strips
- 5 cloves
- 10 allspice berries
- 3 cardamom pods, bruised using a rolling pin
- 2 bay leaves
- 2 cinnamon sticks
- 100ml calvados, apple or regular brandy

Directions:

1. Put all the ingredients except the calvados in a slow cooker pot and cook for 1 hr on high or up to 4 hrs on low.
2. Just before serving, stir in the calvados. Ladle into heatproof glasses or cups to serve.

Nutritional Value (Amount per Serving):

Calories: 84; Fat: 0.69; Carb: 21.69; Protein: 0.62

Chapter 8: Desserts

Air Fryer Apricot And Raisin Cake

Prep Time: 10 Minutes
Cook Time: 12 Minutes   Serves: 8

Ingredients:

- 75g dried apricots
- 4 tbsp orange juice
- 75g self-raising flour
- 40 g Sugar
- 1 egg
- 75g Raisins

Directions:

1. Preheat air fryer to 160°C.
2. In a blender or food processor blend the dried apricots and juice until they are smooth.
3. In a separate bowl, mix together the sugar and flour.
4. Beat the egg. Add it to the flour and sugar. Mix together.
5. Add the apricot puree and raisins. Combine together.
6. Spray an air fryer safe baking tin with a little oil. Transfer the mixture over and level off.
7. Cook in the air fryer for 12 minutes, check it at 10 minutes. Use a metal skewer to see if it is done. If need be, return the cake to the air fryer to cook for a few more minutes to brown up.
8. Allow to cool before removing from the baking tin and slicing up.

Nutritional Value (Amount per Serving):

Calories: 95; Fat: 1.37; Carb: 18.8; Protein: 2.58

Air Fryer Chocolate Brownies

Prep Time: 10 Minutes
Cook Time: 20-25 Minutes   Serves: 16

Ingredients:

- Air fryer
- Air fryer baking tin
- 1 pack brownie mix
- 3 Tablespoons vegetable oil
- 75ml water
- 1 medium egg

Directions:

1. Pour the brownie mix into a bowl then add the water, vegetable oil and egg. Mix it thoroughly and ensure the mixture doesn't have any lumps.
2. Grease the air fryer baking tin and spread the mixture around to get a consistent level throughout.
3. Set the air fryer to 160°C and let the brownies cook for 20-25 minutes. Stick a knife into the brownie and if it comes out almost clean the brownies should be finished.
4. Allow to cool off then slice up into squares and enjoy your air fried brownies.

Nutritional Value (Amount per Serving):

Calories: 204; Fat: 9.44; Carb: 29.74; Protein: 2.13

Air Fryer Fruit Scones

Prep Time: 5 Minutes
Cook Time: 10 Minutes   Serves: 4

Ingredients:

- 120 g self-raising flour
- A pinch of salt
- 40 g butter
- 20 g sultanas
- 20 g sugar
- 75 ml semi-skimmed milk

Directions:

1. Pre-heat your air fryer if needed, to 200°C.
2. Mix flour and butter together until you have a breadcrumb like consistency. Add a pinch of salt.
3. Mix in the sultanas. Then stir the sugar in.
4. Add milk.
5. Mix.
6. Divide into 4.
7. Line your air fryer basket with parchment paper.
8. Drop the mixture in. You can either go for drop scones or you can just add 5g more flour for a dryer consistency (if needed) and use a cutter.
9. Cook for 8-10 minutes at 200°C. Use a cake tester to ensure they're cooked through before serving.

Nutritional Value (Amount per Serving):

Calories: 1014; Fat: 54.4; Carb: 61.1; Protein: 69.41

Air Fryer Pizookie

Prep Time: 5 Minutes
Cook Time: 5 Minutes   Serves: 8

Ingredients:

- Cookie dough recipe:
- 135 g salted room temperature butter
- 70 g light brown sugar
- 70 g sugar
- 10 ml vanilla extract
- 1 egg
- 225 g of plain flour
- 1/2 tsp teaspoon bicarbonate of soda
- 175 g chocolate chunks or chocolate chips

Directions:

1. Combine together the butter and both sugars in a bowl.
2. Add the egg and vanilla extract once combined.
3. In a separate bowl mix together the flour, bicarbonate of soda and chocolate chunks/chocolate chips.
4. Combine the wet and dry ingredients in a bowl and mix together until just

combined.

5. Once the dough is mixed roll it out into a circular shape, wrap in clingfilm and then chill for a minimum of 1 hour. You can leave it overnight if you'd prefer. Chilling like this helps for a chewier more delicious cookie.

6. Add the dry ingredients to the wet ingredients and mix until combined well.

7. If you're in a hurry you could skip the chilling, but I really feel it adds to the overall texture of the cookies so try to make time for this step!

8. I like to make either 4 mini pizookies with this dough OR one large one, that will serve 8 people comfortably.

9. Take your chilled cookie dough, roll it out and then shape it to fit either a cake pan or a cast iron skillet. Personally I love to use a well seasoned cast iron skillet, as I feel this gives a great result with a chewy cookie with a well cooked bottom.

10. Pre-heat your air fryer to 180°C for 1-2 minutes if you'd like. I like to do this so the air fryer is ready to go right away.

11. Add your skillet, cake pan, or even just the dough to a baking paper lined air fryer basket, and then cook for 5 minutes at 180°C.

12. Remove from the air fryer and then transfer to a wire cooling rack to cool down.

13. If you used parchment paper then gently peel this back once it's cooled lightly and it'll keep for 2-3 days.

Nutritional Value (Amount per Serving):

Calories: 531; Fat: 21.62; Carb: 58.7; Protein: 5.23

Air Fryer Peanut Butter Cookies

Prep Time: 4 Minutes
Cook Time: 4 Minutes   Serves: 20

Ingredients:

- 250 g smooth peanut butter
- 250 g white caster sugar
- 1 egg

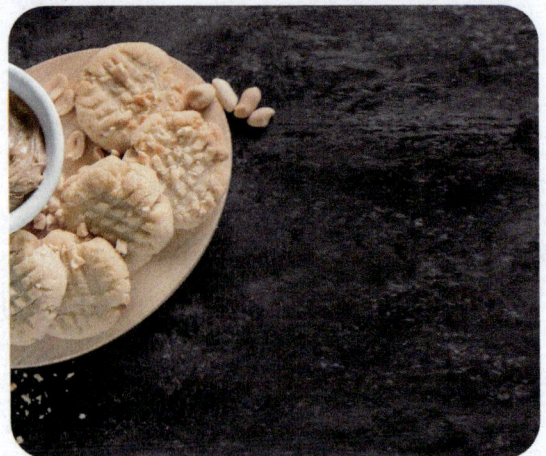

Directions:

1. Mix together the ingredients until you've got a smooth consistency. Try not to overwork the mixture.

2. Line your air fryer basket with baking paper. You can use reusable baking paper if you have this instead.

3. (If you're going to make multiple batches like I do then you'll want to

measure the baking paper before you heat up the air fryer, cut your paper and then you'll have it all to hand ready to line with the cookie dough before placing into the basket carefully to avoid burning yourself).

4. Place walnut sized balls of the dough on to the baking paper.
5. Press down lightly with a fork or spoon, depending on whether you want the little cut indentations or not.
6. Cook at 200°C for 4 minutes. Check at the 2 minute mark just to ensure the dough balls haven't moved together as air flow can be very strong in some air fryer models.
7. You want to remove these when they are just lightly golden brown to avoid burning them.
8. Depending on your air fryer model you may want to add another 1-2 minutes of cook time. I use the OL750UK and this heats up VERY fast!
9. Remove from the air fryer basket and leave to cool on a wire rack. I like to just remove the parchment paper using a spatula, carefully, and then individually transfer to the wire rack from there. This works great when cooking multiple batches, which I usually am.

Nutritional Value (Amount per Serving):

Calories: 109; Fat: 8.58; Carb: 6.79; Protein: 2.15

Air Fryer Dessert Pizza

Prep Time: 5 Minutes
Cook Time: 5 Minutes   Serves: 8

Ingredients:

- 1 pizza base
- 150 ml chocolate spread
- 150 g strawberries
- Mint to garnish

Directions:

1. Oil the air fryer basket lightly.
2. Take your pizza base, or rolled out pizza dough, and place it into the lightly oiled air fryer basket.
3. Cook this undressed pizza base at 200°C for 5 minutes until it is lightly cooked.
4. While this is cooking wipe over and remove the tops from your strawberries. Then slice your strawberries either in half or into thinner slices to lay across the cooked base.
5. Leave to cool slightly for a few minutes on a cooling rack.

6. Spread across the chocolate spread. The residual heat from the base will melt this and make it easier to spread.
7. Add your strawberries and spread across in a nice pattern.
8. Add a mint garnish.
9. Slice and serve.
10. See above for more topping suggestions.

Nutritional Value (Amount per Serving):

Calories: 3116; Fat: 167.06; Carb: 356.4; Protein: 42.65

Air Fryer Chocolate Chip Cookies

Prep Time: 10 Minutes
Cook Time: 35 Minutes   Serves: 1

Ingredients:

- 115 g butter, melted
- 55 g brown sugar
- 50 g caster sugar
- 1 large egg
- 1 tsp. pure vanilla extract
- 185 g plain flour
- 1/2 tsp. bicarbonate of soda
- 1/2 tsp. salt
- 120 g chocolate chips
- 35 g chopped walnuts

Directions:

1. In a medium bowl whisk together melted butter and sugars. Add egg and vanilla and whisk until incorporated. Add flour, bicarbonate of soda, and salt and stir until just combined.
2. Place a small piece of parchment in the basket of an air fryer, making sure there is still room around the edges to allow air flow. Working in batches, use a large cookie scoop, about 3 tablespoons, and scoop dough onto parchment, leaving 5cm between each cookie, press to flatten slightly.
3. Bake in air fryer at 180°C for 8 minutes. Cookies will be golden and slightly soft. Let cool 5 minutes before serving.

Nutritional Value (Amount per Serving):

Calories: 2537; Fat: 123.78; Carb: 330.06; Protein: 30.64

Air Fryer Brownies

Prep Time: 5 Minutes
Cook Time: 30 Minutes   Serves: 2

Ingredients:

- 100 g caster sugar
- 40 g cocoa powder
- 30 g plain flour
- 1/4 tsp. baking powder
- Pinch salt
- 60 g butter, melted and cooled slightly
- 1 large egg

Directions:

1. Grease a 15cm round cake pan with cooking spray. In a medium bowl, whisk to combine sugar, cocoa powder, flour, baking powder, and salt.
2. In a small bowl, whisk melted butter and egg until combined. Add wet ingredients to dry ingredients and stir until combined.
3. Transfer brownie batter to prepared cake pan and smooth top. Cook in air fryer at 180°C for 16-18 minutes. Let cool 10 minutes before slicing.

Nutritional Value (Amount per Serving):

Calories: 931; Fat: 57; Carb: 92.15; Protein: 14.37

APPENDIX RECIPE INDEX

Printed in Great Britain
by Amazon